BIZARRE BEAST B

RAT VS. COCKROACH

Gareth Stevens
PUBLISHING

By Charlotte Herriott

Please visit our website, www.garethstevens.com. For a free color catalog of all our high-quality books, call toll free 1-800-542-2595 or fax 1-877-542-2596.

Library of Congress Cataloging-in-Publication Data

Herriott, Charlotte, author.
 Rat vs. cockroach / Charlotte Herriott.
     pages cm. — (Bizarre beast battles)
 Includes bibliographical references and index.
 ISBN 978-1-4824-2788-2 (pbk.)
 ISBN 978-1-4824-2789-9 (6 pack)
 ISBN 978-1-4824-2790-5 (library binding)
1. Rats—Juvenile literature. 2. Cockroaches—Juvenile literature. 3. Animal behavior—Juvenile literature. 4. Animal weapons—Juvenile literature. I. Title. II. Title: Rat versus cockroach. III. Series: Bizarre beast battles.
 QL737.R666H48 2015
 599.35'2—dc23
                                        2014049886

First Edition

Published in 2016 by
Gareth Stevens Publishing
111 East 14th Street, Suite 349
New York, NY 10003

Copyright © 2016 Gareth Stevens Publishing

Designer: Katelyn E. Reynolds
Editor: Therese Shea

Photo credits: Cover, p. 1 (rat) Tom McHugh/Science Source/Getty Images; cover, p. 1 (cockroach) Aleksey Stemmer/Shutterstock.com; cover, pp. 1–24 (background texture) Apostrophe/Shutterstock.com; pp. 4–21 (rat icon) yyang/Shutterstock.com; pp. 4–21 (cockroach icon) Ksanawo/Shutterstock.com; p. 4 photobobs/Shutterstock.com; pp. 5, 21 (rat) Heiko Kiera/Shutterstock.com; p. 6 seeyou/Shutterstock.com; p. 7 Barnaby Chambers/Shutterstock.com; pp. 8, 14 Emi/Shutterstock.com; p. 9 kzww/Shutterstock.com; p. 10 Astrid Riecken For The Washington Post/Getty Images; p. 11 nuwatphoto/Shutterstock.com; p. 12 DEA/A. Calegari/Getty Images; p. 13 Constantin Falk/Getty Images; p. 15 CHOKCHAI POOMICHAIYA/Shutterstock.com; p. 16 William Lombardo/The Image Bank/Getty Images; p. 17 Bates Littlehales/National Geographic/Getty Images; p. 18 David J. Sams/The Image Bank/Getty Images; p. 19 Candy Hall/Shutterstock.com; p. 21 (cockroach) skynetphoto/Shutterstock.com.

Printed in the United States of America

CPSIA compliance information: Batch #CS15GS: For further information contact Gareth Stevens, New York, New York at 1-800-542-2595.

CONTENTS

Words in the glossary appear in **bold** type the first time they are used in the text.

REALLY GROSS RATS

Rats! Eek! There are 56 kinds, or species, of animals called rats. All have a slim body, a pointed head, furry ears, and a long tail. Brown rats and house rats especially have spread throughout the world wherever people live. People provide rats with food—whether they mean to or not!

Many homeowners fear rats as carriers of **disease**. Disease can spread through the waste rats leave behind. Rats also chew easily through house **materials**. They can do a lot of harm wherever they're found.

RATS HAVE SHARP CLAWS FOR DIGGING AND CLIMBING.

5

CREEPY COCKROACHES

What makes people squirm as much as rats? Cockroaches! There are about 4,000 species of cockroaches around the world. These insects have a flat, oval body, long antennae, and three pairs of legs. Males usually have two pairs of wings, too. However, most species don't fly well.

Just a few species of cockroaches are the pests people may see in their homes. Like rats, cockroaches leave behind waste that can spread disease. And like rats, they seem to be wherever people are, easily traveling in bags and boxes.

COCKROACHES HARM MORE MATERIALS THAN THEY EAT. THEY GIVE OFF A GROSS SMELL, TOO!

SIZE SIDE-BY-SIDE

Imagine if these two pests, rats and cockroaches, faced off in a battle to the death. Who would win? Let's compare size first. Rats can be many different sizes. The largest species of rat is the Sulawesian white-tailed rat.

WEIGHT: UP TO 8.5 OUNCES (241 G)

LENGTH: AS LONG AS 10 INCHES (25 CM), WITH A TAIL OF SIMILAR LENGTH

WEIGHT:
UP TO 1 OUNCE (28 G)

LENGTH:
UP TO 3 INCHES (8 cm)

Cockroaches can be different sizes, too. The largest species is called the rhinoceros cockroach. They can live 10 years! All rats are longer and heavier than even the heaviest cockroach. They win this contest easily!

SPEEDING PESTS

Rats and cockroaches might be easier to get rid of if they weren't so fast. Rats have long legs. They run on all fours, using their tail for balance. Rats can run up walls, too!

TOP SPEED:
6 MILES (9.7 KM) PER HOUR

Rats can't run upside down on **ceilings** like cockroaches can, though. Cockroaches' long back legs push them forward—and fast. If cockroaches were as big as people, they'd be running 200 miles (322 km) per hour! But they're small, thankfully. Rats are faster and can catch cockroaches.

HIDE-AND-SEEK

Rats are excellent at hiding and make their homes in small spaces, such as under rocks and in woodpiles, underground dens, **attics**, drawers, and **cabinets**. Anywhere there's food nearby is a good place to set up home for a rat.

CAN FIT INTO:
1/2-INCH (1.3 cm) SPACE

Cockroaches can be hard to find because they like fitting into supertight spaces, even a space as thin as a dime! They seem to like squeezing their body into small spaces. Even if a rat could find the cockroach, could it get the insect out of its hiding place?

SURPRISINGLY TOUGH

Rats are pretty tough. They may build up and pass down **immunity** to certain poisons to their children. They can swim ½ mile (0.8 km), and they've been known to scare off house cats! Here are some other amazing **survival** features.

SURVIVAL FEATURE:
CAN FALL FROM A GREAT HEIGHT WITHOUT INJURY

SURVIVAL FEATURE:
CAN GO LONGER WITHOUT DRINKING WATER THAN A CAMEL

SURVIVAL FEATURE:
CAN LIVE FOR A MONTH WITHOUT FOOD

Cockroaches are known as some of the toughest creatures on Earth. Most animals need their brain to live, but not the cockroach! A rat would die without its head right away. The cockroach takes this round of toughness!

15

HOW SMART?

Both rats and cockroaches are considered "smart" in some ways. Let's see who wins in a battle of **intelligence**.

HOW SMART?
OFTEN COME UP WITH UNEXPECTED **STRATEGIES** IN TESTS

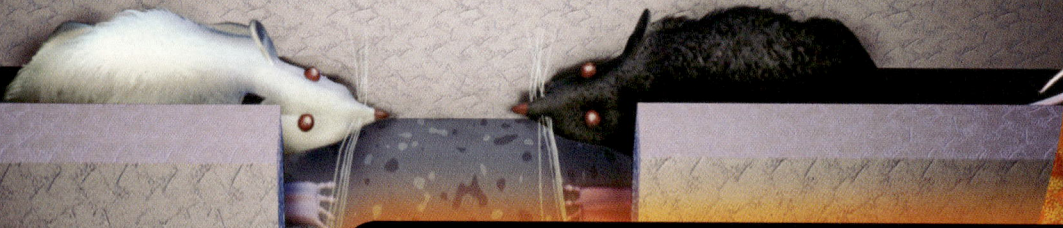

HOW SMART?
USE SEVERAL SENSES TO MAKE DECISIONS

Scientists know that cockroaches can learn, though they aren't exactly sure how. They also know that the insect has a memory. Rats are likely smarter than cockroaches. They seem to have the ability born in them, as opposed to being taught by scientists.

17

TEETH VS. MANDIBLES

Rat teeth grow 5 inches (12.7 cm) a year. They have to keep **grinding** them down. Rats have no problem chewing on nonfood items, such as paint, soap, leather, cloth, glue, and even their own poop!

CAN CHEW THROUGH:
WOOD, BRICK, CONCRETE, METAL

CAN CHEW THROUGH:
CARDBOARD, THIN PLASTIC, CLOTH

Cockroaches have **mandibles** for cutting and grinding. You might think as long as you don't have food lying around, you won't have a cockroach problem. They also eat grease, soap, books, hair, and their own babies! But rats definitely have the tougher teeth. And rats definitely eat cockroaches!

19

THE WINNER?

So who'd win in a fight, a rat or a cockroach? Before you say "rat," remember that a cockroach could survive even if the rat bit off its head—at least for a time! And a cockroach could certainly find a place to hide where a rat couldn't find it.

Both are enemies of people, and their numbers are increasing each year. A pair of rats may have as many as 2,000 babies. Cockroaches can produce a colony of 800 to 300,000! Both animals will be around to battle for a long time to come.

BOTH RATS AND COCKROACHES HAVE SHORT LIVES. RATS USUALLY LIVE 2 TO 3 YEARS. COCKROACHES LIVE A FEW MONTHS TO ABOUT 2 YEARS.

GLOSSARY

attic: a room or space that is just below the roof of a building and often used to store things

cabinet: a piece of furniture that is used for storing things and usually has doors and shelves

ceiling: the overhead inside lining of a room

disease: illness

evolve: to grow and change over time

grind: to use a rough surface to shape or smooth something

immunity: the power to keep oneself from being affected by a disease

intelligence: the ability to learn skills and apply them

mandible: a mouthpart of insects or arachnids used to bite or hold food

material: something used to make something, such as cloth

strategy: a plan of action to achieve a goal

survival: living through something

FOR MORE INFORMATION

BOOKS

Bodden, Valerie. *Cockroaches.* Mankato, MN: Creative Paperbacks, 2014.

Claybourne, Anna. *Rats.* Chicago, IL: Raintree, 2013.

Rebman, Renee C. *Rats.* New York, NY: Marshall Cavendish Benchmark, 2012.

WEBSITES

How Cockroaches Work
animals.howstuffworks.com/insects/cockroach.htm
Find out everything you need to know about cockroaches.

20 Things You Didn't Know About . . . Rats
discovermagazine.com/2006/dec/20-things-rats
Read some interesting facts about these four-legged creatures.

INDEX